FRENCH FLOWERS

Giftwraps by Artists

Geschenkpapier von Künstlerhand

Papiers cadeau d'artistes

A Joost Elffers Book

h.f.ullmann

© 2011 for this edition Tandem Verlag GmbH
h.f.ullmann is an imprint of Tandem Verlag GmbH

Special edition

Text: Susan Meller
Translation into German: Brigitte Wünnenberg
Translation into French: Arnaud Dupin de Beyssat

Editor: Eric Himmel
Designer: Darilyn Lowe
Photography: Les Morsillo

Layout: Yvonne Schmitz
Cover: Simone Sticker

Overall responsibility for production: h.f.ullmann publishing,
Potsdam, Germany

Printed in Austria

ISBN 978-3-8331-6325-8

10 9 8 7 6 5 4 3 2 1
X IX VIII VII VI V IV III II I

www.ullmann-publishing.com
newsletter@ullmann-publishing.com

Bibliography • Bibliographie
Clouzot, Henri, and Morris, Frances: *Painted and Printed Fabrics.*
New York, 1927
Clouzot, Henri: *Histoire de la manufacture de Jouy et de la toile imprimée
en France.* C. van Oest, Paris et Bruxelles, 1928
Durant, Stuart: *Ornament.* London, 1986
Journal of Design. London, 1849–52
Robinson, Stuart: *A History of Printed Textiles.* London, 1969
Tuchscherer, Jean-Michel: *The Fabrics of Mulhouse and Alsace, 1801–1850.*
Leigh-on-Sea, England, 1972
Pitoiset, Gilles: *Toiles imprimées XVIIIe-XIXe siècles.* Société des Amis de la
bibliothèque Forney, Paris, 1982
Heutte, René: *Les Étoffes d'ameublement.* H. Vial, Paris, 1980

The production of textiles is and always has been one of the largest industries in the western world. The processes involved in the weaving and printing of cloth, from the preparation of the raw materials to the subsequent manufacturing of garments and home furnishings, are so complex and the number of supporting industries so vast that,

Typical French block-printed indienne fabric of the late eighteenth century, probably by Oberkampf.

Typisches Beispiel für einen französischen Indienne-Stoff des späten 18. Jhs. – vom Druckstock, wahrscheinlich von Oberkampf.

Cette indienne imprimée à la planche, probablement réalisée par Oberkampf, est caractéristique du style français de la fin du XVIIIᵉ siècle.

directly or indirectly, a huge portion of the world's economy depends on the textile industry. Millions of people are employed in it; mills must be kept running; cloth must be woven and printed; and products manufactured. What will turn the plain cloth, or gray goods as unfinished print cloth is called, into fashion? Designs. Textile designs must be created season after season, through good times and bad, in

Die Textilherstellung ist immer einer der größten Industriezweige der westlichen Welt gewesen. Angefangen bei der Vorbereitung der Rohstoffe bis hin zur anschließenden Herstellung von Kleidungsstücken und Dekorationsstoffen, sind die Arbeitsgänge des Webens und Stoffdrucks so komplex und die Zulieferindustrien so zahlreich, dass ein großer Teil der Weltwirtschaft direkt oder indirekt von der Textilindustrie abhängt. Sie beschäftigt Millionen von Menschen; Spinnereien und Webereien müssen in Betrieb gehalten werden. Stoffe müssen gewebt und bedruckt, schließlich die Endprodukte angefertigt werden. Was verwandelt den einfachen Stoff oder die „Grisette", wie noch nicht bedrucktes Tuch genannt wird, in Mode? Dekors. Saison für Saison, in guten wie in schlechten Zeiten, müssen neue Textildekors kreiert werden, damit diese riesige Maschinerie in Gang bleibt.

Die Textildekors in diesem Band wurden in Frankreich während der letzten zwei Dekaden des 19. und zu Beginn des 20. Jhs. gemalt. Sie stehen in der Tradition der großartigen Blumenmotive, die den Ruhm französischer Designer begründeten. Selbst ihre Hauptkonkurrenten, die Engländer, erkannten deren Überlegenheit an. Schließlich schaute seit dem 18. Jh. die ganze Welt auf Frankreich, wenn es um Fragen der Mode und Gestaltung ging. Der technische Fortschritt, die aktive Rolle des Königs bei der Förderung der gestaltenden Künste und die künstlerische Kultur der Nation trugen zur Führungsposition Frankreichs auf diesen Gebieten bei.

Die französische Textildruck-Industrie hatte ihre Wurzeln im 17. Jh. und resultierte aus der Nachfrage der Bevölkerung nach farbechten, fröhlich gemusterten Stoffen, wie sie zur damaligen Zeit nur aus Indien zu bekommen waren, und durch das Gesetz, das sie ihnen verwehrte. 1686 gab die französische Regierung dem

L'industrie textile est et a toujours été une des plus importantes du monde occidental. Les techniques utilisées pour le tissage et l'impression, depuis la préparation de la matière brute jusqu'à la confection des toiles et des tissus d'ameublement, sont si complexes et le nombre des activités qui lui sont liées, directement ou indirectement, si important qu'une grande partie de l'économie mondiale dépend de cette seule industrie. Elle emploie en effet des millions de personnes pour faire tourner les filatures sans arrêt, tisser et imprimer les étoffes et

A paper impression of a design for indienne fabric, which served as a printer's proof to test the block before the actual printing on cloth. France, late eighteenth century, probably by Oberkampf.

Papierdruck eines Motivs für indiennes, ein Probeabzug zur Überprüfung des Druckstockes vor dem eigentlichen Bedrucken des Gewebes. Frankreich, spätes 18. Jh., wahrscheinlich von Oberkampf.

L'impression sur papier d'un motif d'indienne servait d'épreuve de contrôle de la planche gravée avant l'impression sur la toile. France, fin du XVIIIᵉ siècle, probablement d'Oberkampf.

order to keep this enormous machine moving forward.

The textile designs in this book were painted in France during the last two decades of the nineteenth century and the early years of the twentieth. They follow in the tradition of great floral patterns for which French designers became renowned. Even their major competitors, the English, regarded the French designers as superior to their own. Indeed, beginning in the eighteenth century, the world looked to France as the leader in fashion and design. Technical developments, the active role of the king in encouraging the decorative arts, and the artistic culture of the nation all played a role in French ascendancy in these fields.

The textile printing industry in France had its roots in the seventeenth century and grew out of the population's desire for colorfast, gaily patterned cloth, which at that time was available only from India, and the subsequent law which denied it to them. In 1686, the French government, under mounting pressure from domestic textile producers, passed a law forbidding the importation, wearing, and use of Indian painted cotton cloth. (The Indian term for this fabric was "chittes," later Anglicized to chintz). These brightly colored fabrics covered with exotic flowers, which had been popular before the ban, became an obsession afterwards. For the next one hundred years "indiennes," as the French called them, were the height of fashion. People disregarded the law and continued to smuggle the cloth into France. Gentlemen entertained guests at home dressed in long robes of indienne fabric called banyans. Large cotton panels painted with fantastic tree-of-life patterns were hung on walls, or used as bed covers and hangings. These panels, known as "palampores," represented the height of Indian textile dyeing and painting achievements. The central motif, a twisted tree blooming with

zunehmenden Druck einheimischer Textilhersteller nach und verbot die Einfuhr, das Tragen und die Verwendung bemalter indischer Baumwollstoffe. (Der indische Begriff für diese Gewebe war „chittes", anglisiert wurde daraus später Chintz.) Daraufhin wurden diese leuchtend bunten, mit exotischen Blumen geschmückten Stoffe, die sich schon vor dem Verbot so großer Beliebtheit erfreut hatten, geradezu eine Obsession. Während der nächsten 100 Jahre waren „indiennes", wie die Franzosen sie nannten, die große Mode. Man missachtete das Verbot und schmuggelte die begehrten Stoffe weiterhin nach Frankreich. Angetan mit langen Gewändern aus „indienne", den sogenannten Banyans, empfingen Herren der besten Gesellschaft ihre Gäste. Große, mit fantastischen Lebensbaum-Motiven bemalte Baumwolltücher wurden als Wandbehang, Bettüberwurf oder Vorhänge verwendet. Diese als „palampores" bekannten Stoffbilder stellten die Blüte indischer Textilfärbe- und Textilmalkunst dar. Das zentrale Motiv war ein gewundener, mit übergroßen Fantasieblüten bedeckter Baum, zwischen dessen Ästen sich häufig noch exotische Vögel, Schmetterlinge, Eichhörnchen und andere Tiere tummelten. Die Franzosen des 17. Jhs. hatten nie zuvor eine solche Flora und Fauna gesehen und waren vollkommen bezaubert.

Christophe-Philippe Oberkampf war der Vater der französischen Textildruck-Industrie. 1760 gründete er seine berühmte Manufaktur in Jouy, vor den Toren von Paris. Sie entstand mit dem Ziel, die nach wie vor stark gefragten indiennes herzustellen. Im Gegensatz zu anderen kleinen Manufakturen jedoch, die schlicht indische Importe kopierten, häufig mit wenig haltbaren, schnell verblassenden Farben, heuerte Oberkampf herausragende Künstler an und schuf seine eigenen Originalmuster. Seine Chemiker entwickelten ständig bessere Farben und Drucktech-

fabriquer les produits finis. Toutefois, le tissu écru, c'est-à-dire non apprêté, ne deviendra un objet de mode que grâce aux dessins qui vont l'enrichir. Ce sont ces créations qu'il faut renouveler saison après saison quelles que soient les circonstances pour satisfaire en permanence le goût du public et permettre à cette énorme machine industrielle de tourner.

Les dessins pour étoffes reproduits dans cet ouvrage ont été exécutés en France entre 1880 environ et les premières années du XXe siècle. Ils poursuivent la tradition des grands motifs floraux qui avait fait la renommée des dessinateurs français et suscitait même l'admiration jalouse des Anglais, leurs grands concurrents dans le domaine des dessins pour étoffes. La France était

A hand-painted cotton palampore made in India about 1760 for the European export trade.

Handgemalter palampore aus Baumwolle, um 1760 in Indien für den Export nach Europa gefertigt.

Palampore de coton peint à la main réalisé en Inde vers 1760 pour le marché européen.

oversize fantasy flowers, often had exotic birds, butterflies, squirrels, and other animals cavorting among its branches. Seventeenth century Frenchmen had never seen such flora and fauna before and it totally captivated them.

The father of the French textile printing industry was Christophe Philippe Oberkampf. In 1760, he founded his famous factory in Jouy, just outside of Paris. It was set up to produce indiennes, which were still very much in demand. Unlike other small manufacturers who simply copied the Indian imports, often with "non-fast" dyes that quickly faded, Oberkampf hired fine artists and created his own original patterns. His chemists were continually developing better dyes and printing techniques. Samuel Widmer, a nephew of Oberkampf and a pupil of the famous chemist Claude Berthollet, invented the first solid green dye in 1808. Up until then, green could only be produced by printing yellow and then blue over it, or vice versa. It was a major break-through for the industry. Oberkampf's colors were light- and water-fast and, like the Indian mordant-dyed cloth, retained their brilliance. So exquisite was his finished cloth that it was worn by the members of the courts of Louis XV and Louis XVI and used to decorate the royal residences.

Dutch flower still lifes like this one, painted by Jan van Huysum in 1736, were a source of inspiration for the lush floral textile designs of the nineteenth century.

niken. Samuel Widmer, ein Neffe Oberkampfs und Schüler des berühmten Chemikers Claude Berthollet, erfand 1808 die erste beständige grüne Farbe. Bis dahin konnte man Grün nur erzeugen, indem man zuerst Gelb druckte und es dann mit Blau überlagerte oder umgekehrt. Oberkampfs Farben waren lichtecht und wasserbe-ständig; seine Waren behielten wie die indischen, mit kaustischen Farben bemalten Stoffe ihre Leucht-kraft. Seine fertigen Stoffe waren so exquisit, dass sie am Hofe Ludwigs XV. und Ludwigs XVI. ge-tragen wurden und die königlichen Residenzen schmückten. Es gelang Oberkampf, seine Landsleute mit diesen im Inland hergestellten indiennes zufriedenzustellen. Alle von ihm gedruckten Muster waren so erfolgreich, dass in vielen anderen europäischen Ländern große Nachfrage nach seinen Textilien bestand. Als Napoleon 1806 die Oberkampf-Manufaktur besichtigte, zeigte er sich so beeindruckt, dass er den Orden der Ehrenlegion von seiner eigenen Brust nahm und ihn Oberkampf persönlich anheftete. Der Vorfall fand weitreichende Beachtung, und aus allen Teilen Frankreichs trafen Glückwünsche für den neuen „légionnaire" ein. Vier Jahre später kam Napoleon erneut nach Jouy. Nachdem er über eine Stunde mit der Betrachtung der schönsten Stoffe des Unternehmens verbracht hatte, orderte er bei Oberkampf die

Holländische Blumenstilleben wie dieses Gemälde von Jan van Huysum (1736) waren eine Inspirationsquelle für die auf-wendigen Blumenmotive der Textil-industrie des 19. Jhs.

Ce genre de nature morte hollandaise, celle-ci peinte par Jan van Huysum en 1736, fut une source d'inspiration impor-tante pour les luxuriants dessins floraux réalisés au XIXᵉ siècle.

en effet considérée dès le XVIIIᵉ siècle. comme le chef de file mondial en matière de mode et de style. Les progrès techniques, le rôle actif du roi pour encourager les arts décoratifs et la culture artistique de la nation jouèrent un rôle capital pour affirmer la suprématie française dans le domaine esthétique.

L'industrie de l'impression textile en France plonge ses racines au XVIIᵉ siècle. Elle doit son développement au désir qu'avait la population de disposer de ces étoffes grand teint ornées de motifs de couleurs gaies qui n'étaient à l'époque fabriquées qu'en Inde et dont l'entrée fut légalement interdite en France en 1686. En effet, sous la pression appuyée des tisserands et des soyeux, le gouvernement français promulgue deux édits royaux interdisant l'importation, l'usage et le port de calicots imprimés (le terme indien désignant ce tissu est «chite», devenu chintz en anglais). Très appréciées avant ces mesures, ces toiles peintes très colorées, à motifs de fleurs exotiques, font désormais l'objet d'une extraor-dinaire passion. Au siècle suivant, l'utilisation des «indiennes» est le comble de la mode. La loi est ouvertement bafouée et la contrebande des toiles s'organise en France. Les gentilshommes se font alors un plaisant devoir de recevoir leurs hôtes vêtus de longues robes de toile indienne appelées banians, dans un décor où d'immenses cotonnades peintes de fantastiques rinceaux d'arbre de vie étaient tendues sur les murs, jetées en guise de dessus-de-lit ou disposées en rideaux. Le motif général de ces toiles imprimées, appelées «palampores» et considérées comme parmi les plus belles réalisations indiennes en matière de dessin et de teinture sur étoffes, présentait un arbre contourné aux branches ornées de fleurs géantes de fantaisie et où folâtraient oiseaux, papillons, écureuils et autres animaux exotiques. De telles images ne pouvaient que ravir les Français du XVIIᵉ siècle, qui n'avaient

Oberkampf succeeded in satisfying his countrymen with these domestically produced indiennes. Indeed, he was so successful with every style he printed that his textiles were in demand in many other European countries. When Napoleon visited the Oberkampf factory in 1806, he was so impressed that he took the Legion of Honor medal off his own breast and personally pinned it onto Oberkampf. The act was widely reported and congratulations from all parts of France were sent to the new "légionnaire." Four years later Napoleon again arrived in Jouy. After spending over an hour viewing the most beautiful fabrics of the establishment, he ordered Oberkampf to bring to him at St. Cloud a selection of his finest indiennes so that he might give them as gifts to the ladies of his court. It was on that visit that Oberkampf was given a private audience with the Emperor. It has been reported that Napoleon said to Oberkampf, "You and I wage good war on the English, you by your industry and I by my armies. But yours is the most effective."

Like the artists retained by Oberkampf, Jean-Baptiste Huet, Mlle. Jouanon, and Peter, the best designers of the nineteenth century were also master flower painters, many of whom were trained as academic artists at the École des Beaux-Arts in Paris, which emphasized draftsmanship, the copying of classical art, and direct rendering from nature. Beginning in 1673, the king of France sponsored regular juried exhibitions, or salons, of work by artists who belonged to the Académie Royale de Peinture (later the École des Beaux-Arts). The system, which rewarded the efforts of traditionally trained artists, in large part survived the French Revolution, and provided a good livelihood and social prestige to those who participated in it. As a practical matter, the Académie and the standards it established contributed to France's export trade by raising the quality of her products. Among the artists who

Lieferung einer Auswahl der feinsten indiennes nach St. Cloud; die Stoffe waren als Geschenke für die Damen seines Hofes bestimmt. Während dieses Besuches erhielt Oberkampf eine Privataudienz beim Kaiser. Berichten zufolge sagte Napoleon zu Oberkampf: „Sie und ich führen einen guten Feldzug gegen die Engländer, Sie mit Ihrer Industrie und ich mit meinen Armeen. Allerdings ist Ihrer der effektivere."

Wie die von Oberkampf beschäftigten Künstler – Jean-Baptiste Huet, Mlle Jouanon und Peter – waren die besten Zeichner des 19. Jhs. zugleich auch meisterhafte Blumenmaler. Viele von ihnen hatten die akademische Malweise an der École des Beaux-Arts (Akademie der Schönen Künste) in Paris erlernt, wo man großes Gewicht auf Zeichenkunst, das Kopieren klassischer Werke und die realistische Abbildung der Natur legte. Seit 1673 fanden unter der Schirmherrschaft des Königs von Frankreich regelmäßige Ausstellungen, die Salons, mit Preisverleihung statt. Teilnehmen konnten Künstler, die der Académie Royale de Peinture (Königliche Akademie für Malerei, die spätere École des Beaux-Arts) angehörten. Dieses System, das die Bemühungen traditionell ausgebildeter Künstler belohnte, überdauerte größtenteils auch die Französische Revolution und bedeutete für alle Teilnehmer gute Einkünfte und hohes gesellschaftliches Ansehen. Als praktische Konsequenz förderten die Académie und die von ihr festgelegten Standards Frankreichs Export, indem sie für eine Qualitätssteigerung der Produkte sorgten. Zu den Künstlern, die im ausgehenden 19. Jh. aufwendige Motive für Dekorationsstoffe schufen, gehörten der für seine großen Blumenbouquets berühmte Jean-Ulric Tournier, Jacques Schaub, Charles Bloesch und Georges Zipélius.

Die Engländer wiederum, denen nur zu bewusst war, wie sehr es

jamais vu auparavant une flore et une faune aussi fabuleuses.

Le père de l'imprimerie textile française est Christophe-Philippe Oberkampf. En 1760, il fonde la célèbre manufacture de Jouy-en-Josas, près de Paris, pour y produire des «indiennes», un style d'étoffe alors encore très demandé. Contrairement aux autres petites fabriques, qui se contentaient de copier les tissus importés des Indes et de les imprimer avec une teinture de moins bonne qualité qui passait rapidement, Oberkampf engage des artistes accomplis et crée ses propres motifs tandis que ses chimistes inventent des teintures et des techniques d'impression meilleures. En 1808, Samuel Widmer, neveu d'Oberkampf et élève du célèbre chimiste Claude Berthollet, met ainsi au point le premier véritable vert, qu'on ne pouvait obtenir jusque là qu'en imprimant successivement du jaune et du bleu. Cette découverte est un progrès majeur pour toute l'industrie textile. Les couleurs créées par Oberkampf sont stables à la lumière et résistantes à l'eau et, à l'exemple des toiles indiennes teintes par des colorants à mordant, conservent toute leur brillance. Ces étoffes étaient si délicates qu'elles furent adoptées à la cour de Louis XV et de Louis XVI et utilisées dans la décoration des résidences royales. Si Oberkampf connaît un véritable succès auprès de ses compatriotes grâce à ses indiennes «françaises», ses impressions dans différents styles étaient si réussies qu'il obtient également des commandes en provenance de nombreux autres pays européens. Lorsque Napoléon visite la manufacture de Jouy en 1806, il est si impressionné qu'il récompense solennellement Oberkampf en lui agrafant sa propre médaille de la Légion d'Honneur sur la poitrine. Ce geste vaut au nouveau «légionnaire» les félicitations de tous. Revenant à Jouy quatre ans plus tard, Napoléon s'attarde encore plus d'une heure à admirer les étoffes produites par la manufacture et commande aussitôt à Oberkampf de lui apporter au château de Saint-Cloud une

created sumptuous designs for home furnishing fabrics in the latter part of the nineteenth century were Jean-Ulric Tournier, famous for his large floral bouquets, Jacques Schaub, Charles Bloesch, and Georges Zipélius.

Textile design sketch after Jan van Huysum. France, second half of the nineteenth century.

Skizze für ein Textildekor nach Jan van Huysum. Frankreich, 2. Hälfte des 19.Jhs.

Étude de bouquet d'après Jan van Huysum. France, seconde moitié du XIXᵉ siècle.

The English, on the other hand, acutely aware of their lack of trained and talented designers, decided to compete with the French by establishing schools of design supported by the government. The first of these schools were opened in 1837. Twelve years later 16,000 pupils had passed through the schools, yet only a handful were gainfully employed as textile designers. The schools were not succeeding with their goal of raising the quality level of British designs. In part it was due to poor management, but the real reason probably lies in the prevailing attitude of the English textile manufacturers, summed up in this remark

ihnen an talentierten und gut ausgebildeten Textilgestaltern mangelte, beschlossen, mit Frankreich in Wettstreit zu treten, indem sie von der Regierung geförderte Schulen für Gestaltung gründeten; die ersten wurden 1837 eröffnet. Zwölf Jahre später hatten 16.000 Studenten eine solche Ausbildung absolviert, doch nur eine Handvoll von ihnen arbeitete als Textilgestalter. Ihr Ziel, das Qualitätsniveau britischer Designs zu heben, konnten diese Schulen nicht erreichen, zum Teil aufgrund ihrer unzureichenden Verwaltung. Die eigentliche Ursache lag jedoch wahrscheinlich in der herrschenden Einstellung der englischen Textilindustrie, wie sie 1849 vom Besitzer einer großen Glasgower Stoffdruckerei zum Ausdruck gebracht wurde, als er vor einem Untersuchungsausschuss zum Scheitern der Schulen erklärte: „Die Franzosen geben den Geschmack vor, und wir folgen ihnen. Ich fahre drei- oder viermal im Jahr nach Paris, nur um Muster einzukaufen und zu sehen, was die Franzosen machen."

Wie heute waren auch die Textilzeichner des 19. Jhs. entweder in einem bestimmten Atelier angestellt, oder sie arbeiteten als Freischaffende. Die meisten, wenn nicht sogar alle Motive in diesem Buch entstammen Pariser Ateliers. Sie tragen so namhafte Stempel wie Atelier Arthur Martin, Atelier Eugène Wolfsperger, Atelier Jacob und Atelier Pollet; keines dieser Ateliers existiert mehr. Sie entwickelten hauptsächlich Dekors für die Textilindustrie, und da Tapetenmuster eng damit verbunden waren, arbeiteten sie häufig auch für diesen Markt. Die fertigen Produkte wurden nicht von ihnen hergestellt. Ihre Aufgabe bestand darin, kreative Ideen zu liefern und diese Ideen so auf Papier zu bringen, dass es technisch möglich war, sie auf Stoffe zu übertragen. Ihre Klientel waren die Textildrucker, die solche Muster auswählten, von denen sie glaubten, sie in Form bedruckter

sélection de ses plus belles indiennes pour les offrir aux dames de sa cour. C'est à l'occasion d'une audience au cours de cette visite que l'empereur aurait dit à Oberkampf: «Vous et moi faisons la guerre aux Anglais, vous par votre industrie et moi par mes armées. La vôtre est certes plus efficace.»

À l'instar des artistes engagés par Oberkampf – Jean-Baptiste Huet, Mᶦᶦᵉ Jouanon et Peter – les meilleurs dessinateurs du XIXᵉ siècle sont également des maîtres en peinture florale, la plupart ayant été formés de manière académique à l'École des Beaux-Arts de Paris, où l'accent est mis sur le dessin, la copie des œuvres classiques et l'interprétation directe de la nature. Dès 1673, le roi de France parrainait des salons, c'est-à-dire des expositions régulières où étaient présentées les œuvres des artistes de l'Académie Royale de Peinture (future École des Beaux-Arts). Ce système récompensant les peintres formés de manière traditionnelle survécut à la Révolution et continua de leur offrir de bons moyens d'existence et un certain prestige social. D'un point de vue pratique, l'Académie et les normes qu'elle définissait contribuèrent, grâce à l'amélioration des produits, au développement des exportations françaises d'étoffes imprimées. Jean-Ulric Tournier, célèbre pour ses grands bouquets de fleurs, Jacques Schaub, Charles Bloesch et Georges Zipélius comptent, à la fin du XIXᵉ siècle, parmi les principaux auteurs des plus beaux dessins pour les tissus français d'ameublement.

Les Anglais, de leur côté, parfaitement de manquer jusqu'à présent de dessinateurs bien formés et talentueux, décident de concurrencer les Français en créant des écoles de dessin financées par le gouvernement. Les premières écoles ouvrent leurs portes en 1837. Douze ans plus tard, elles ont accueilli 16 000 élèves, dont seuls quelques-uns ont obtenu un emploi rémunéré de dessinateur dans l'industrie textile. Si ces écoles n'ont pas atteint

made in 1849 by the owner of a large Glasgow printworks before a committee investigating the failure of the schools: "The French lead the taste, and we follow them. I go to Paris three or four times a year for no other purpose than to buy designs and see what the French are doing."

Like today, the "nineteenth-century" designers were either employed by a particular studio (atelier), or worked on a freelance basis. Most, if not all, of the designs in this book originated in Parisian studios. They bear the stamp of such studios as Atelier Arthur Martin, Atelier Eugène Wolfsperger, Atelier Jacob, and Atelier Pollet, none of which are in business today. The studios were concerned mainly with developing patterns for the textile industry, and as wallpaper patterns were closely related, they would often design for that market as well. They did not manufacture the finished product. Their function was to provide creative ideas and to render those ideas on paper in a way that was technically possible to reproduce on cloth. Their clients were the textile printers, who would choose designs which they felt they in turn could sell to their customers in the form of printed yard goods. Once a design was purchased, the studio was usually asked to paint it again to the client's specifications. That meant putting it into the proper repeat size so that the engraver at the textile mill was able to engrave directly from it. Usually several different color combinations, or colorways, were required, so the studio artist would do that as well by painting a representative portion of the design in each colorway, based on the needs of the client.

The artists who created the designs in this book were among the thousands of anonymous artists whose works we still use today—as patterns on our clothes, walls, bedding, and floors. They belong to an industry whose creative force comes mainly from the brushes of ghost artists. History records few of their names. We know

Meterware an ihre Kunden verkaufen zu können. Hatte ein Kunde ein Muster erworben, bat er das Atelier gewöhnlich, es nach seinen Vorgaben erneut zu malen. Das bedeutete, es auf das richtige Größenverhältnis zu bringen, damit der Graveur in der Textilfabrik direkt nach der Vorlage arbeiten konnte. Gewöhnlich waren mehrere verschiedene Farbkombinationen gefordert; folglich führte der Atelierkünstler auch diese aus, indem er einen repräsentativen Abschnitt des Musters in jeder Farbkombination malte, entsprechend den Wünschen des Kunden.

Die Grafiker, von denen die Motive in diesem Buch stammen, zählen zu den Tausenden anonymer Künstler, deren Werk wir noch heute verwenden – als Muster auf unserer Kleidung, unseren Wänden, unserer Bettwäsche und unseren Fußböden. Sie haben ihre Kreativität unerkannt in den Dienst eines Industriezweigs gestellt und die Kunstgeschichte kennt nur wenige von ihnen mit Namen. Einige ihrer Ateliers sind uns bekannt, hauptsächlich durch die Stempel auf der Rückseite ihrer Entwürfe. Sind diese jedoch einmal auf Stoff gedruckt, verschwindet jede Spur ihres Ursprungs.

Die Muster wurden in Gouache-Technik gemalt – opaken, wasserlöslichen Farben, die damals wie heute das vorrangige Medium für das Textildesign darstellen. Praktisch in der Anwendung, kommt ihre Wirkung dem Aussehen der im Stoffdruck verwandten Pigmente sehr nahe. Die Motive wurden für den Innenausstattungsmarkt entworfen. Der mit ihnen bedruckte Stoff fand vorrangig Verwendung für Vorhänge, Polsterstoff und als Bezug für Daunenfederbetten. Während damals bedruckte Bettlaken vollkommen unbekannt waren, besaß jeder Haushalt der Mittel- und Oberschicht Federbetten, die gewöhnlich mit dicht gewebten, bedruckten Baumwollstoffen bezogen waren. Großformatige,

leur objectif d'améliorer le niveau de qualité des dessins britanniques, cela est dû en partie à leur mauvaise gestion mais très probablement aussi à l'attitude des industriels anglais du textile, que résume cette remarque faite en 1849 par le propriétaire d'un grand atelier d'impression de Glasgow devant la commission d'enquête chargée précisément d'enquêter sur l'échec de ces écoles: «Les Français font la mode, et nous les suivons. Je me rends à Paris trois ou quatre fois par an sans autre but que d'acheter des dessins et voir ce que font les Français.»

Les dessinateurs du XIXe siècle étaient, comme aujourd'hui, soit employés dans un atelier soit travailleurs indépendants. La plupart sinon tous les dessins de cet ouvrage proviennent d'ateliers parisiens et portent le tampon des ateliers Arthur Martin, Eugène Wolfsperger, Jacob ou Pollet (aucun n'existe plus aujourd'hui). Ces ateliers s'occupaient essentiellement de créer des motifs pour l'industrie textile mais aussi pour les fabricants de papiers peints, de techniques très proches. Ils n'avaient en revanche aucun rôle dans la fabrication, se contentant de proposer des créations et de les exprimer sur papier de manière à ce qu'il soit techniquement possible de les reproduire sur tissu. Les imprimeurs sur étoffe leur achetaient alors les dessins qui leur semblaient le mieux convenir à leur clientèle. Une fois le principe du dessin acquis, on demande généralement à l'atelier de le refaire suivant les spécifications de l'imprimeur, c'est-à-dire de le reproduire à un format permettant sa répétition en motifs et sa gravure sur plaque. Comme l'impression se faisait généralement dans plusieurs combinaisons de couleurs, l'artiste doit également peindre un échantillon représentatif du dessin dans chacun des coloris proposés aux clients.

Les artistes qui ont créé les dessins reproduits dans cet ouvrage font partie de ces milliers d'artistes anonymes dont les œuvres sont

some of their studios, mainly from the stamp on the back of their designs. But once on cloth, the source all but disappears.

The patterns were executed in gouache, an opaque, water-based paint, which was, and still is, the primary medium for textile designs. It is practical to use and simulates most closely the look of the pigments used to print cloth. They were designed for the home furnishing market. The most popular use for the finished cloth would have been curtains, upholstery, and covers for down quilts. While printed sheets were unheard of in those days, every middle- and upper-class home had down coverlets which were usually covered in a tightly woven printed cotton. Large-scale, sumptuous florals were a favorite choice for that purpose, and the designs in this book, which have been scaled down for giftwraps, would have been widely used.

After the designs were painted to the specifications of the manufacturer, they were sent to the mill to be engraved. If the pattern were to be block printed, it would have been necessary to carve it by hand into wooden blocks. Usually pear wood was used as it was extremely hard and had a fine grain. A separate block would have been required for each part of the pattern which was a different color. Block printing was done by hand by highly skilled workers who carved the blocks and printed the cloth. It was much more time-consuming and expensive than roller printing. By the end of the nineteenth century, most of the fabrics produced for mass consumption were roller printed. If the design were to be roller printed, it was then transferred by means of a pantograph to a large copper roller. Each color in the pattern required a separate roller: if there were twelve different colors it would be necessary to engrave twelve rollers. Today roller printing has for the most part been replaced by rotary screen printing, but up until the 1970s it was still widely used. At that

aufwendige Blumenmotive waren besonders beliebt, und die Muster in diesem Buch waren daher weitverbreitet; für Geschenkpapier wurden sie ebenfalls in kleinerem Maßstab reproduziert.

Nachdem die Entwürfe genau nach den Angaben der Manufaktur gemalt worden waren, sandte man sie zum Gravieren in die Fabrik. War das Muster für den Blockdruck bestimmt, musste es per Hand in hölzerne Druckstöcke geschnitten werden. Dafür nahm man gewöhnlich wegen seiner Härte und feinen Maserung Birnbaumholz. Für jede Farbe mussten die entsprechenden Teile des Musters in einen gesonderten Druckstock geschnitten werden. Das Drucken vom Holzschnitt war reine Handarbeit, wobei hoch qualifizierte Handwerker die Druckstöcke schnitten und das Gewebe bedruckten. Diese Technik war viel zeitraubender und kostspieliger als der Walzendruck. Daher wurden Ende des 19. Jhs. die meisten massenproduzierten Stoffe mit der Walze bedruckt. War die Zeichnung für die Walze bestimmt, übertrug man sie mithilfe eines Pantografen auf eine große Kupferwalze. Jede Farbe des Musters erforderte eine eigene Walze: Bei zwölf verschiedenen Farben mussten also zwölf Walzen graviert werden. Heute hat der Rotations-Siebdruck größtenteils den Walzendruck verdrängt, bis in die 1970er-Jahre war er jedoch noch weitverbreitet. Damals druckte man gewöhnlich mit maximal sechs Walzen pro Muster. Um die Jahrhundertwende jedoch waren Muster wie die in diesem Band durchaus nicht selten, die mit 15 oder sogar mehr Farben gedruckt wurden. Die Technik hatte einen so hohen Perfektionsgrad erreicht, dass die Qualität des auf Stoff gedruckten Motivs der des gemalten Entwurfs gleichkam.

Das Muster wurde von den Walzen auf eine Vielzahl unterschiedlicher Gewebe gedruckt, einschließlich Samt, Satin, Rips, Damast, Moiré, Chintz, Popeline,

encore reproduites de nos jours – sur nos vêtements, nos murs, nos lits et nos sols. Ils appartiennent à une industrie dont la force est née du pinceau créateur de ces artistes, restés bien souvent inconnus de l'histoire. Si nous connaissons quelques-uns de leurs ateliers, c'est grâce essentiellement au tampon qui figure à l'envers des dessins, dont les originaux ont d'ailleurs presque tous disparus une fois imprimés.

Les motifs étaient exécutés à la gouache, une peinture à l'eau opaque qui reste le principal médium pour les dessins sur étoffe car il est d'utilisation pratique et peut imiter parfaitement l'aspect des pigments employés pour l'impression sur tissu. Ces étoffes étaient destinées au marché de la décoration d'ameublement: rideaux, tapisseries et courtepointes. Dans les demeures des bourgeois et des aristocrates, les draps imprimés n'existant pas, la literie était en effet dissimulée sous un vaste édredon de duvet enveloppé d'une housse de coton piqué, ornée de préférence de vastes et somptueux motifs floraux (parmi lesquels certains des dessins présentés dans ce livre et mis à l'échelle pour servir de papier cadeau).

Les dessins repris en peinture suivant les spécifications du fabricant sont alors expédiés à la filature où ils sont gravés sur des planches de poirier – un bois apprécié pour son extrême dureté et la finesse de son grain, qui sera progressivement remplacé par le cuivre – à raison d'une planche pour chaque partie du dessin imprimée dans une couleur particulière. Ce mode d'impression, exécuté à la main par des ouvriers hautement qualifiés, étant très long et bien plus cher que l'impression au rouleau, la plupart des tissus produits en quantité sont imprimés suivant cette nouvelle technique dès la fin du XIXᵉ siècle. Dans ce cas, on transfère le dessin sur de grands rouleaux de cuivre à l'aide d'un pantographe, chaque couleur à imprimer nécessitant, là encore, la gravure d'un rouleau distinct; pour un motif

time, six was generally the maximum number of rollers used for one pattern. But at the turn of the nineteenth century, it was not unusual to find designs, like the ones in this book, printed with fifteen or more colors. The technical achievements were so high that the quality of the printed design on cloth was equal to that of the painting.

The design was printed from the rollers onto a variety of fabrics, including velvet, satin, reps, damask, moiré, chintz, poplin, granité, and cretonne. Cotton was the most common cloth for printing, but occasionally wool, silk, or linen was used as well. Many color combinations were produced, often as many as a dozen different colorings of each pattern. Usually the pattern was printed on several fabrics and each one was printed in a set of colorings. If a design were printed in ten color combinations on six kinds of cloth, the sample booklet of that design would contain sixty examples of it–all different! The theory of the manufacturers was to give their customers the widest possible choice and let no taste go unsatisfied. Even today, European textile printers offer their clients a wider range of patterns and colorings than do their American counterparts. In the USA, the emphasis has always been on printing long runs, 10,000 yards and up of a particular pattern. While the days of the "million yarder" are mostly in the past, 100,000 yards of a design is a realistic expectation for an American textile printer.

While the designs in this book were originally purchased from Parisian studios, the actual cloth was printed in Alsace, primarily in Mulhouse and several surrounding towns. Alsace has been one of the most important textile printing centers in France from the beginning of the nineteenth century until today. The region had a turbulent history, bouncing back

Wollkrepp und Cretonne. Der gebräuchlichste Stoff für den Druck war Baumwolle, gelegentlich wurden aber auch Wolle, Seide oder Leinen verwendet. Man stellte zahlreiche Farbkombinationen her, oft bis zu einem Dutzend pro Muster. Normalerweise druckte man ein Muster auf mehrere Stoffarten, wobei für jedes Gewebe eine ganze Palette von Farbkombinationen hergestellt wurde. Wenn also ein Motiv in zehn Farbkombinationen auf sechs unterschiedliche Stoffarten gedruckt wurde, enthielt das Musterbuch 60 Variationen dieses einen Dekors! Es gehörte zur Strategie der Hersteller, ihren Kunden die größtmögliche Auswahl zu bieten und keine Geschmacksrichtung unberücksichtigt zu lassen. Noch heute bieten europäische Textildrucker ihren Kunden eine größere Auswahl an Mustern und Farben als die Hersteller in Amerika, wo das Hauptgewicht immer auf der Produktion langer Stoffbahnen von mindestens 10.000 Yards (9.144 m) eines bestimmten Musters lag. Der „million yarder" gehört zwar fast der Vergangenheit an, doch 100.000 Yards (91.440 m) von einem Muster liegen durchaus im Rahmen der realistischen Erwartungen eines amerikanischen Textildruckers.

Während die Motive in diesem Buch ursprünglich aus Pariser Ateliers stammen, wurde der Stoff im Elsass bedruckt, hauptsächlich in Mulhouse und einigen umliegenden Städten. Das Elsass ist seit Anfang des 19. Jhs. eines der wichtigsten Zentren des französischen Textildrucks. Der Region war eine turbulente Geschichte beschieden, sie erlebte einen stetigen Wechsel zwischen Unabhängigkeit, französischer und deutscher Herrschaft.
In der Entstehungszeit dieser Designs gehörte das Elsass zum deutschen Herrschaftsgebiet, nachdem Frankreich es 1870/71 in einem kurzen Krieg zwischen Napoleon III. und dem Fürst von Bismarck, dem preußischen Reichskanzler unter Wilhelm I.,

en 12 couleurs, il faut donc graver 12 rouleaux de cuivre. Ce procédé, remplacé depuis par la sérigraphie, a été largement employé jusque dans les années 1970. À cette époque, on n'utilisait plus que six rouleaux au maximum pour un dessin mais, au tournant du XIXe siècle, il n'était pas rare que les impressions, comme celles de cet ouvrage, soient réalisées en 15 couleurs ou plus. La technique avait déjà évolué à un point tel que le motif imprimé sur le tissu était de qualité très comparable à la peinture originelle.

Le dessin une fois gravé peut alors être imprimé sur l'étoffe, aussi variée que le velours, le satin, le reps, le damas, le moiré, le chintz, la popeline, le granité ou la cretonne. Le coton est la matière la plus utilisée mais laine, soie et lin sont également employés. Les impressions sont ensuite réalisées sur plusieurs types d'étoffe et dans différents coloris, souvent une douzaine pour chaque motif. De ce fait, s'il est prévu de l'imprimer dans dix coloris sur six sortes d'étoffes, le livre d'échantillons qui sera constitué présentera alors 60 exemples différents du même motif, les fabricants étant désireux d'offrir à leurs clients le choix de tissus le plus vaste possible. Aujourd'hui encore, les imprimeurs de tissus européens proposent une gamme plus étendue de motifs et de coloris que leurs concurrents américains. En effet, l'accent a toujours été mis aux États-Unis sur l'impression en grande série, c'est-à-dire sur des métrés de 10 000 yards (9144 m) et plus, d'un même motif. Si l'époque du «million de yards» est révolue, la réalisation d'un métrage imprimé de 100 000 yards (91440 m) est loin d'effrayer les imprimeurs américains de textiles.

Si les dessins de cet ouvrage proviennent d'ateliers parisiens, les étoffes ont été en revanche imprimées en Alsace, principalement à Mulhouse et les villes avoisinantes. L'Alsace est en effet l'un des plus importants centres d'impression de tissus de France depuis le

and forth between independence, French control, and German control. During the period in which these designs were created, Alsace was under German domain, the French having lost it in 1870/71 after a brief war between Napoleon III and Otto von Bismarck, Prime Minister of King William I of Prussia. This presented the Alsatian textile manufacturers with a difficult dilemma—they had to choose whether to continue producing printed cloth for the French market, or to switch over and supply it to the Germans. If they chose the former, they faced double taxation—duty on the gray goods they imported from France and taxes on the finished cloth they exported. The advantages were that they were dealing with a known market, established accounts, and their own countrymen. If they decided to cater to the German market, there were the obvious financial advantages and the ease of doing business. But the German taste was different than the French. Designs had to be modified, designed, and colored for another market.

These flower paintings in the French taste were printed by a firm which chose to continue doing business with the French. After Alsace was returned to France in 1918, this firm prospered and, in fact, is still in business today, printing lovely floral patterns. Its neighboring competitor, who chose to produce for Germany, never recovered after World War I and has since ceased textile printing.

The designs on these pages were produced at the same time as those of the Arts and Crafts and Art Nouveau movements. However, unlike the latter two, whose highlystylized motifs appealed to a more sophisticated taste level, these designs were intended for the mass market and were commercially far more successful and widely used. They remain as popular today as they were a century ago.

verloren hatte. Diese Tatsache stellte die elsässischen Textilhersteller vor ein schwieriges Problem – sie mussten sich entscheiden, ob sie weiterhin bedruckte Stoffe für den französischen Markt herstellen oder sich umstellen und ihre Ware für die Deutschen produzieren sollten. Blieben sie bei ihrer bisherigen Produktion, stand ihnen doppelte Besteuerung ins Haus – Einfuhrzoll auf die „Grisette", die sie aus Frankreich importierten, und Ausfuhrzoll auf die Fertigwaren, die sie exportierten. Die Vorteile waren, dass sie auf einem vertrauten Markt, mit einem etablierten Kundenstamm und ihren eigenen Landsleuten Handel treiben konnten. Beschlossen sie dagegen, den deutschen Markt zu bedienen, brachte das die offensichtlichen finanziellen Vorteile und einfach abzuwickelnde Geschäfte. Der Geschmack der Deutschen unterschied sich jedoch von dem der Franzosen. Die Motive mussten für einen neuen Markt abgewandelt, neu entworfen und koloriert werden.

Die hier vorgestellten Blumenmotive im französischen Stil wurden von einer Firma gedruckt, die sich entschied, ihre Geschäfte mit Frankreich fortzuführen. Nachdem das Elsass 1918 an Frankreich zurückgefallen war, florierte das Unternehmen; es existiert noch heute und druckt weiterhin wunderschöne Blumenmuster. Das benachbarte Konkurrenzunternehmen, das beschlossen hatte, für Deutschland zu produzieren, konnte sich nach dem Ersten Weltkrieg nicht erholen und stellte seinen Betrieb ein.

Die Dekors in diesem Band entstanden gleichzeitig mit den Arbeiten der „Arts and Craft"-Bewegung in England und des Art nouveau, deren stilisierte Motive allerdings anspruchsvollere Geschmäcker ansprachen. Im Gegensatz dazu waren diese Muster für einen breiten Markt gedacht, kommerziell weitaus erfolgreicher und weiter verbreitet. Sie sind heute noch ebenso beliebt wie vor 100 Jahren.

début du XIXᵉ siècle. Cette région a connu une histoire mouvementée, au cours de laquelle elle est passée alternativement de l'indépendance au contrôle français ou allemand. À l'époque où ces dessins ont été créés, l'Alsace appartient à l'Allemagne, qui l'a annexée après la guerre de 1870/71 entre Napoléon III et Bismarck, le chancelier de Guillaume Iᵉʳ de Prusse. Cette situation posait un dilemme aux fabricants alsaciens de tissus: continuer à produire des tissus imprimés pour le marché français, ou fournir le marché allemand. S'ils choisissaient la première solution, ils devaient supporter une double imposition des frais de douane sur les tissus écrus importés de France et une taxe sur les textiles finis à l'exportation; l'avantage est qu'ils travaillaient sur un marché et avec des clients connus. S'ils décidaient de travailler avec les Allemands, il bénéficiaient d'avantages financiers et de facilités de commerce, mais le goût allemand étant différent de celui des Français, il fallait reprendre, modifier et réimprimer en d'autres couleurs les dessins qu'ils existants.

Ces peintures de fleurs au goût français étaient imprimées par une entreprise qui choisit de continuer de travailler avec les Français. Après la restitution de l'Alsace à la France en 1918, cette entreprise a prospéré et, toujours en activité, continue d'imprimer de délicieux motifs floraux. Son concurrent et voisin, qui avait alors choisi l'Allemagne, n'a jamais pu reprendre une activité suffisante à la fin de la Première Guerre mondiale et a cessé depuis l'impression de tissus.

Les dessins de ces pages ont été réalisés à l'époque des mouvements Arts & Crafts et Art nouveau. Cependant, contrairement aux œuvres de ces deux mouvements, dont les motifs très stylisés s'adressaient à un public aux goûts plus sophistiqués, ces dessins étaient destinés essentiellement à un marché de masse et connurent

Every decade throughout the past two hundred years of commercial textile printing has had its look. But there have been consistent, recurring themes underlying fashion trends. One is flowers. Beautiful flowers. Flowers have been used on fabrics more than any other motif. People instinctively respond to flowers—to their colors, forms, and scent. The symbolism of flowers differs among cultures, but universally they speak to us of beauty, life, and joy. Roses, poppies, anemones, hollyhocks, tulips, primroses, irises, hydrangeas, chrysanthemums, narcissus, crown imperial—as these flowers reappear in nature season after season, so do they appear on the clothes we wear and the fabrics we live with. For the artist, they are a delight to paint. The variety of shapes, textures, and hues provides an infinite source of design inspiration. For the manufacturer, they offer a safe and popular motif which has proven to be continually successful.

Der kommerzielle Textildruck entwickelte während der letzten zwei Jahrhunderte in jedem Jahrzehnt einen eigenen Stil. Allen Moderichtungen zum Trotz hat es jedoch immer beständige, wieder-kehrende Themen gegeben. Blumen sind ein solches Thema. Wunderschöne Blumen. Häufiger als jedes andere Dekor sind Blumenmotive auf Stoffe gedruckt worden. Der Mensch reagiert instinktiv auf Blumen – auf ihre Farben, Formen, Düfte. Die Symbolik der Blumen ist von Kultur zu Kultur unterschiedlich, sie sprechen jedoch überall zu uns über Schönheit, Leben und Freude. Rosen, Mohnblumen, Anemonen, Malven, Tulpen, Primeln, Iris, Hortensien, Chrys-anthemen, Narzissen, Kaiserkrone – sie alle kehren Jahr für Jahr in die Natur zurück, und ebenso er-scheinen sie auf den Kleidern, die wir tragen, und den Stoffen, in die wir uns hüllen. Für den Künstler ist es eine Freude, sie zu malen. Die Vielzahl ihrer Formen, Strukturen und Farbnuancen bildet eine unerschöpfliche Inspi-rationsquelle für die Gestaltung. Dem Textilhersteller bieten sie ein sicheres und beliebtes Motiv, das sich als dauerhaft erfolgreich erwiesen hat.

d'ailleurs une bien meilleure réussite commerciale. Ils sont aujourd' hui encore aussi populaires qu' il y a une centaine d'années.

Si les toiles peintes ont connu des styles variables sur des cycles d'une dizaine d'années au cours des deux siècles passés, on remarque cependant des thèmes récurrents capables de perdurer en dépit des tendances de la mode, notamment les compositions florales. Les motifs de fleurs ont en effet enrichi les tissus plus que tous les autres. Tout le monde apprécie les fleurs – leurs couleurs, leurs formes et leurs odeurs – et si le symbolisme des fleurs diffère selon les cultures, elles nous parlent toutes de beauté, de vie et de plaisir. Roses, coquelicots, anémones, roses trémières, tulipes, primevères, iris, hortensias, chrysanthèmes, narcisses apparaissent chaque année sur les vêtements que nous portons et les tissus dans lesquels nous vivons tout comme elles s'épanouissent dans la nature à chaque saison. Pour l'artiste, elles sont un sujet agréable à peindre pour les ressources infinies d'ins-piration qu'offre la diversité de leurs formes, de leurs textures et de leurs couleurs. Pour l'imprimeur d'étoffes, elles sont un motif populaire qui garantit un succès sans cesse renouvelé.